Remedies for Vertigo

Remedies for Vertigo

Poems by Walter Bargen

Cherry Grove Collections

Published by Cherry Grove Collections
P.O. Box 541106
Cincinnati, OH 45254-1106

Typeset in Palatino by WordTech Communications
LLC, Cincinnati, OH

ISBN: 193345640X
LCCN: 2006930709

Poetry Editor: Kevin Walzer
Business Editor: Lori Jareo

Visit us on the web at www.cherry-grove.com

The following poems first appeared in:

American Letters & Commentary: "Red Shift"
Beloit Poetry Journal: "Flying the Flat World"
Chester H. Jones Anthology (1995): "The Right Nurture,
    The Left Nature"
88: "End Time," "No Where"
Farmer's Market: "To Keep Going"
Fresh Ground: "Tooled"
Green Hills Literary Lantern: "On a Good Day," "The
    Unmistaken"
Heliotrope: "Superman's Suicide"
Icarus Press Anthology: "Problems with the Holy," "The
    Rising Flocks," "Explanation," "Sparrows"
Laurel Review: "Dialects," "Concessions"
Meridian: "Breakfast with Asteroids"
Missouri Review: "At a Glance," "Walking on Air"
Montserrat Review: "USA"
New Letters: "Experiments in Flight"
Pleiades: "The Civilized Sacrifice"
Rattle: "Southern Perfection," "Minor Gods"
Redaction: "Centenarian," "Bears on the Roof"
River Styx: "Photographing the Wind"
Rockhurst Review: "Kite"
Sow's Ear Poetry Review: "Acid Rain"
Willow Springs: "The Freight of Parakeets"

"How He Died" won the Chester H. Jones Foundation
Award in 1997. "The Civilized Sacrifice" also appears
in the anthology *Knowing Stones.*

For Bobette: more furred than feathered.

Contents

Walking on Air

Pinioned

1
Fly I said throwing him into the air.
        —W.S. Merwin

2
. . . and all the birds are suspended in flight . . .
        —Mark Strand

3
Some evenings we saw solitary men and women
floating above the dark tree tops.
        —Charles Simic

Flying on Instruments

Experiments in Flight

1 Playing Chicken

When his mother sent him to catch a chicken
strutting in the yard, he knew not to walk
directly toward any one of the flock pecking
and scratching amid the weeds and tireless cars
mounted on concrete blocks. He must act
as if he were headed in another direction,
and only coincidentally walking past
toward the shed for a shovel or to the storm cellar
for potatoes, all the time edging ever-so-slightly
sideways while staring straight ahead, but really
watching from the corner of his eye, then springing
and bending in one scooping motion into his arms,
a squawking, flapping chicken, then holding it
at arm's length by its scaly, clawed feet. It wasn't
that "eat or be eaten" wasn't clear to him,
but that he'd never wrung their necks the way
his mother had shown him; he squeezed the air out
of them, as if holding a feathered bag pipe
under his arm, their jabbing beaks turning
in a slow, dizzying motion until the last note
died away and they hung limp. He loved to show off
to passing neighbor kids, how he was old enough
to pluck the world of its terrified notes.

2 Incubating Souls

It's an experiment conducted late in the school year,
close to Easter, when the crocuses are blossoming
low to earth's green blush that hasn't been beaten
bald by tennis shoes taking the shortcut
between sidewalks back to class after the bell
has ended recess. There are two cardboard boxes,
stacked on a table at the back of the room
where the coats hang low to the tiled floor
like wrinkled souls yet to rise. A fine mesh screen
stretches between the stacked boxes.
A bare bulb in the bottom one heats the eggs
day and night. There's a viewing flap cut
into one side. Perhaps it was simply the incubator,
too large and airy, or that every kid in the class
kept running to the back to check, imagining
the coming cracks in this new world, bored
with their drawings of cuddly hatchlings
taped to the walls. They let in too much cold,
a few eggs weren't fertilized, and when the teacher
returned from spring break the air in the room
was so overpowering she nearly doubled over
before slamming the door. An hour later,
after the janitor had left, after the lunch boxes
were lined along the wall, the attendance taken,
the class wanted to know why the windows were
open–not yet ready for a calamitously cool spring.

3 Mocking

The stars refuse to come closer
the way they have other nights.
He squints harder. They just shimmer
and float farther away as he lies
on the bed staring out the window.
He gives up, listens. Each belch,
cat call, rasp, screech,
is a wall of sound that builds
then tumbles over the sill into his room
before fading into soft rubble
at the bottom of a seamless dark.
If there were no birds, no grinding
gears, no neighbors arguing
and threatening to shoot each other,
then there would be nothing to
stop him, and he could walk out
of this house. Walled-in he's certain
the world's flat. He's tried flying
off the edge of his mattress.
By morning the walls are higher.
There is a mockingbird perched in
the peach tree outside his window.

4 The Extinction of White Pants

Everywhere: banging into windshields,
hanging between cats' fangs, in heaping
mounds around six-hundred-feet-high
transmission towers, in flattened glyphs
under tires, sticking obliquely in radiator
grills, limp in the hands of crying six-year-
olds, flying through doors into windowless
rooms and stunned by swinging brooms,
angling up sleeves and unbuttoned shirts,
tangling in bouffants, falling in lines along
poisoned roof ridges, entangled in the aching
wires of angry conversations, crowding under
bridges and staining railings, plaguing pedestrians
in the canyons of downtown, their deafening
migratory chatter drowning lakes, their
lofty lines wrinkling the sky—he starts for
work wearing white pants, and on a sharp
turn his coffee cup flies across his lap.

5 Looking for a Way

Nothing else matters, that's all he remembers
upon awakening. In the gray flutter
of dawn he stares out the kitchen window,
hardly noticing the feathered crimson streaks
trailing east as morning takes flight. How corny
he thinks, his own heart's height and width pinioned
by sill and sash. Counting panes, six
or twelve, and if he includes both windows,
eighteen and twenty-four with the storms,
which are not even visible from his angle,
except for the subtle refraction of repeating selves
as he looks for his own flight back into this day.
Yesterday, seated at a table in a city hours away,
his mother told him of another mother
who worked in her son's butcher shop
until she was in her eighties and died one day
at work; so-and-so's husband who played
softball even at his age and swam two miles
daily at the YMCA, who stood up at dinner then
pitched himself across the roast and mash potatoes;
someone else who never regained consciousness
after a heart attack; and so on for the entire meal.
His mother looks for a way into death,
and all he could do is look at her as he does
these kitchen windows, as if nothing else matters,
but beating his wings against the panes.

6 Flying on Instruments

In the flashlight's beam, he follows the frantic
flutter of a dusty brown bird up and down
the shed's cobwebbed window, leaving dusk
streaked with dust and stars. This bird, perhaps
a flycatcher, tries desperately to fly deeper into
night's glittering glass as he approaches and fails
at rescue before grabbing it with one hand
rather than scooping with two. He is surprised
by its weight, or lack of weight, and feels
uncertain how tight to hold a handful of air.
He steps from the door into the dark
and he almost doesn't notice his empty hands.

To Keep Going

Far up the valley,
from deep in the willow thickets
along the creek, a birdcall
comes I don't recognize.

Juan Ramon Jimenez wrote
that he would *go away.*
and the birds will still be
there singing. He was right,

he went away, and some of us
still hear him in the branches
beside our houses
and far up cold creeks.

But there are those birds
that have left too. The last
dusky seaside sparrow died
in a cage behind beach dunes

in Florida, unable to call in a mate.
The shrike, the butcher-bird, Jackie
hangman, the strangler, all names
for feathers on the same bird,

a songbird that goes against the grain
and with hooked beak breaks necks
of mice and other birds and sometimes
hangs their limp bodies on strands

of barbed wire where they dangle
like half-eaten laundry, their song
disappearing too, along with
the meadowlark that has perched on

a fencepost in my garden and tilted its
head back, stretching its neck, exposing
a black feathered necklace as it points
its bill skyward, clearly announcing

spring, a yellow-breasted soloist
fronting an orchestra of greening
grass, it too is going away, and for
no good reason that we understand,

and so there are fewer notes
to remind us of his going.

Concessions

When my son wrestles
his cat into his arms,
    the soft fur is
    suddenly muscled

and clawing, as it struggles
to rescue its instinct. He
    calls and is ignored,
    can't stop calling

as the fledging warbler, wings
outstretched, runs through
    the tomatoes that are hard
    and pale green. I'm

reminded of silent films
where men with wings
    of paper and canvas
    flapped their arms up

and down running across fields,
only to fall off the edge
    of a boulder, a pier, some-
    thing, anything, as if falling

and flying belonged in
the same breath. The cat
    that knows nothing
    else, I tell him to take

into the house, as it
lunges from his arms,
    dives for the faint
    frantic cheeping.

What can I do but catch
the cat, catch the bird,
    exile one to
    the house, one to

a low persimmon branch,
as the parents cry from
    somewhere in the thicket.
    It's a precarious perch

for something so young,
and before I leave
    the tree, the cat is back,
    the door left open.

I see a second fledgling
running down a garden
    row, its half-naked wings
    beating the cold spring air.

Explanation

A child captures a bumblebee,
shows his mother how it sits unperturbed

in his hand, a friend, but she grabs a glass jar
and traps it, screwing the lid on quickly, warning

him not to do it again. There's the beginning
of an incessant rumor that grows louder until

he picks up the jar and bangs it on the ground,
breaking the bottom out, but the bee keeps

ramming the lid, and his mother takes it from
him, sticking the jagged end into the dirt.

Bumblebees, genus *bombus*, order *hymenoptera*,
live in complex colonies, have four membranous

wings, their abdomens attached by slender pedicels.
Hymen is the Greek god of marriage, a vaginal

fold, and lives in our collective love and lust.
This order of insects takes its name

from the fragile union of body parts, of nectar
and air, of diaphanous wings and hymneal

flights, of painful stings and fluttering light,
from boys tumbling through the world.

Kite

In a field shredding light,
his arms outthrust,
fearless, facing the full force,
his paper phoenix ripping skyward,
wind willed, unwillingly
veering left, right,
mad spinning and looping,
diving out of control,
then swooping up
just before the crushing impact.
The kite races higher,
hurdling clouds.

Anchored, grounded,
he feels the taut tension of away,
listens to the seething
unwinding whirl, the tenuous
string of distance playing out.
His fingers burn, trying
to slow the coming end,
hoping the knot will hold.
The spooling handle jerks from his hands,
and bounces across the field.
The kite off wide into the world,
catches on a branch,
before tearing free and apart.

That's what they call them,
paper folded and folded again
until the piece almost disappears
into the lifelines of a palm.
Held so tight they could kill,
these messages passed
between inmates—
scribbled paper kites
sailing through steel bars.

Centenarian

The settling pastels, the walled horizons,
the yellowing nylon curtain pulled back,

unattached to clouds and rain, but the metal
rungs ringing over the guide bar above the bed

are a downpour. The weather
of his room stifling, the day unmoving,

the florescent lights an unsteady flicker. Morning
and evening a switch ruled by experts.

In his morphined daze he dies
and flies over Memphis.

No pyramidal shadows crossing the desert.
No obelisks pointing at sand-stormed skies.

No Blue Nile, no *mastaba*, just a muddy Mississippi
and a convalescent Graceland.

No slave-driven barge,
but a procession of chauffeured pink Cadillacs.

No thronged thousands mourning a sun god,
just a shaky sequined king.

No mummified hawks and crocodiles,
instead porcelain guitar salt and pepper shakers.

No immortal blue yonder.
No wild angelic wonder.

Just a rising cumulus of pain,
a thunderhead jolting every nerve

over Memphis, a pitch and roll
as rain cleanses the room.

—*for Jack Twente*

p-oh-OH-lee

Four pouting syllables, the breezed shuffle of palm leaves,
    the not
quite slipping of sea and season, maybe fine sand between
    fleshy lips,

soft chanting dirge, without a swinging church censer or
    choir or
preacher to call forth the final occasion, just another
    morning starting

the car, driving through coffeed rush hour, attending to
    mall trinkets
and fashions, making arrangements for a plumber,
    lawn care, state

vehicle inspection, not caring, or knowing the open space of
    that now
unsung song in the understory of a canopied rainforest.
    So easy

to overlook the rats, feral pigs, goats, virus-laden mosquitoes,
    all that
we can claim as our manifest destiny, our design and
    desire, ignoring

the little left after who knows how many years, just four
    soft sounds
almost hurting to be spoken, *puo'l.* So few seen,
    identified, spelled

out in that brief flight out of our time. First sighted by
    students, told
to shot, bring back a specimen, and in their hands,
    black-capped,

mostly gray-winged, white-bellied, near weightless, a song
     gone deaf,
the last male dead in a cage at the base of a mid-Pacific volcano

—*puo'l.*

On a Good Day

The one-legged gulls, statuesque on ice, turn their heads,
>   tuck their beaks under feathers along their backs
>   or under an edge of wing. One leg enough to

keep them from sliding off into the water—not good enough
>   for us, even though we watch from shore. Sleepy, crowded
>   together their bellies all point toward the sun.

Occasionally disturbed by a neighbor's refolding of wings,
>   the switching of a cold, tired foot, the fluffing
>   of feathers, these birds, a dozen pillows

piled on ice, invite us to join their melting dreams. The hinge
>   of their voices hardly heard opening the air for anything
>   more than to praise the glory of this warmth.

Two gulls patrol the glistening shrinkage, stopping to cock
>   their heads and examine with one eye
>   the newly exposed half-frozen fish.

The gulls stab and rip thawed pieces of meat. On thin ice
>   on a good day, gulls grow fat. Cold recedes
>   and pale bellyless fish swim free.

Ascension

Acid Rain

Stainless steel bolts slipped from his hands.
He was already balanced on air
and one breath away from his last
as it passed quickly and too easily through
the safety netting. A familiar story,

drinking hard all night, beer for breakfast
to sober up. He held tight to the ladder,
his stretched safety belt an umbilical cord
unwilling to sever into an airborne birth.
The clatter of steel woke him,

his foot slipped back onto a rung.
He watched a silver rain disappear
600 feet below. He didn't hear
their impact or the shouts and curses
of hard-hatted men below. They pulled out

tape measures, probed the holes
in the cinder-packed ground down to three
feet, men who liked to know to the fraction
of the inch how close they came. Engineers
sat around blueprints in the company trailer,

stared through holes in the ceiling,
the ones in the floor, eager to tell what they saw
after work from tailgates and in bars.
From the top of the power plant smokestack,
going higher to disperse the smoky truth

in exchange for the lies of light
and warmth, the man jerks his safety belt
back into place, begins threading
another bolt as he falls through
another hole in the clouds.

Tooled

Body turned on the lathe of hours,
turns each evening into the flat rhythms
of exhaustion. Each morning, night turns
into an interrupted convalescence,
into the harsh angles of day.

Stepping through December, it's windy,
wet, always closing down early.
What can he say, when the man
next to him—they've found
a small surround of sunlight

and little warmth from an idling dozer—
pulls from his wallet a set of worn photographs,
the white of an operating room.
What fell one lunch
from a girdered sky was

an iron-worker's spud wrench,
its handle a foot-long spike.
He lay on the surgical table,
his chest exposed, his face
masked by anesthesia,

the hexagonal end of the wrench perched
on his shoulder like an open-
beaked, greasy-winged parrot.
The handle nested completely inside him.
He was the tool, the tool him,

pierced between clavicle and scapula,
somehow missing heart and lung.
He's pictured in a medical journal.
There's a shadow buried in his body,
the scar stretching from 8 to 5.

History of Flight

Sky an undrained dishwater,
color of the hangover most carry to work
each day, the blunted mind
swaying over the blunted body.

Only a small wedge of light visible
as they descend through morning
deep into blasted excavations.
The odor of cordite clings

to ragged walls. The charge-holes
fume with rock dust.
Freshly splintered strata glistens.
Limestone crowded with the common

litter of seafloor evolution.
In rough pockets sit fist-sized calcite.
They shove crystals into their tool belts,
a punishing weight that bangs against thighs.

The worthless glitter drags
them down as they climb ladders.
Not even pyrite, but they grasp
it with the heart of Forty-niners.

The dozer operator works the pipeline path.
Scraping the floodplain, he's picked up
arrowheads and stone tools.
They know the work can't afford to stop.

A month past skulls rolled
before the shiny blade,
prehistory gravely in the way.
In the backs of trucks, they ride

to long benches and sit
in the shade of a cottonwood.
The noon shift plants dynamite
to excavate the afternoon.

Talk punctuated with muffled concussions.
Coffee shimmers in plastic cups.
In the middle of baloney and lettuce,
a Biblical curse, a rain of dirt and rock.

Head-sized boulders rifle past,
taking-out the legs of chairs,
dropping men to the bare ground,
heaving carpenters onto collapsing tables.

When Bears Fly

1 End Time

Not another ax raised
and swung at the uncleaved
circles of spreading grain.
Not the rhythmic thunk
and crack of wood
echoing across a valley,
timepiece of work and seasons.
Not the shuffling crackle
of winter-brittle weeds.
Not each rough-quartered piece
stacked along a pasture
fence, or a weasel's skinny head
popping out of unstacked logs,
or the slamming screen
door as wood is carried
into the house. Not the clang
of the small cast-iron stove
door as it is opened
and closed to feed the fire,
to keep the heat alive,
the caged, animal-eyed, ember glow
staring back as the handle
is secured shut. Not the scrape
of the shovel scooping ashes
into a metal bucket and hauled
outside to cool before dumping,
or the hiss of a steel brush
cleaning the chimney's
blackened hallway, as if it were
an escape route. None of this,
just the cold growing cold.

2 No Where

No more black, no more white.
No March wind pulling at your hair,
your hat, ballooning pants,
parachuting dresses. No March
or April. No longer a cruelest month.
No fear of the blank page.
Nothing to fill out, no directions to follow.
Nothing to scratch out.
No correction tape.
No last place of employment
and the ten years before that.
No references, nothing referential,
or reverential. No reasons for leaving
or applying. No arriving.
Nothing to lay out: pink shirt, socks,
paisley tie. No bed on which to spread
the luggage's contents, travel alarm clock
and money belt. Not a city, a street,
a wrong address, a stamp to send
a letter. Nothing to forward
or return undeliverable.
Not even a lost letter department.
No passport. No where.

3 Bears on the Roof

Apocalypse passes
without using direction signals.
In overstuffed chairs
we celebrate by drinking
cases of bottled water. It will take
a year to eat all the canned beans.
What were we thinking?

Burn down the outhouse
or leave it for the next tribulation?
Who's going to heft the shovel?
Does a hole ever completely
fill back up?   The grass depression
will be a reminder of what we missed.

The stock of batteries for the radio,
we'll figure out some way
to run them down. Melt
all the candles so they don't fall
into the hands of a satanic cult.
I'm backing up the car
to pump gas from the tanks
behind the shed. The money
buried in the backyard
is already spent on next month's bills.

Back to light switch, microwave,
taking morning showers, hours
of telephone gossip, fighting
rush hour traffic. What's left:
earthquakes, pole reversals,
retreating glaciers, tsunamis,
volcanic eruptions, asteroid collisions,
bears on the roof.

Primitive Flights

1 Muddy Instant

Streets permafrost, more permanent than asphalt.
Earth impenetrable for hundreds of feet. Winter
all but one day of the year oil workers claim,
who dream of retired lives south. Suicides, homicides,
cirrhosis, resignation, the bodies are stored
in a corrugated tin shed beside the church. The entrance
wreathed in caribou antlers. On the day
of the one-day-thaw all work stops: tanning hides,
stringing whale jerky, hunting, fishing, supplying
oil rigs in the bay, repairing snowmobiles. Just a muddy instant:
a few inches of earth shoveled and picked, backhoed deeper,
dynamited if necessary, so the dead can be buried,
and maybe burn down to a warmer place. If relatives can't wait
through months of cold mourning, plane tickets are bought,
and one winter flight south is more dead than alive.

2 Stolen Light

At thirty-seven thousand feet, the jet crosses the last range
of mountains, the demarcation between north and far north,
the difference between two seasons and one, four
a cabalist's invention. Descending he sees the bay
and the slate-flat ocean beyond. It's too cold to walk. He
hails a taxi, a spring green Mercedes. It's the end of the
one day summer: mid-August, sunny with snow flurries.
The driver takes the scenic route. Out the window he sees
a polar bear swimming in the town's sewage lagoon.
They pass a seventy-feet high, oil-drum-welded
sculpture of an oil derrick or the Eiffel Tower. A dusting
of snow at its base points a white shadow north.
Caribou hides nailed to the walls of shacks are more
plentiful than windows. To survive people crawl deep
inside a stolen animal heat. There is desperation
in the air. Each day light freezes fourteen minutes shorter.

3 Drowning North

Congealed cold these fist-sized, ice-shackled rocks thrown up
in heavy surf litter the bay's beach. Wind steady at twenty
miles-an-hour. Sea spray freezes on whatever washes up:
boot, dead seal, coiled barge cables. He picks up a rock
and heaves it back into the waves. Its cold glow visible
all the way to the bottom. At the horizon, the sky turns
solid and sinks into the sea. He searches for signs
of whale migration. Bleak days too early, bleak days too late.
Innuit widen the definition of life,
harpooning the missing, then turn back to town.
A polar bear hide alive with wind flaps against a shack.
He knocks, asks to photograph hide and hunter. The father
returns with his eight-year-old son. They share *muktuk*,
frozen whale blubber: raw, salty, a mouth full of oily, cold sea.

—for Alan Berner

Flying the Flat World

1 Denmark

It's a phenomenal world. The man
sinking in his bathtub knows this.
He calls out for help, the coordinates
somewhere in the Baltic Sea
west of Bornholm Island.
Rescue ships are dispatched
but it's not where the man in the bottle
is floating, soap in his eyes, the water
tepid, even a little cold. Time to turn
the spigot on, regain an amniotic
warmth, hear the water's gurgling
and splash as the turbulent waves
sweep across the deck, one man
already washed overboard and lost,
the claw-legged tub listing forty-five
degrees. How will he ever stand, not slip
on the shifting tiles, grab a towel, hold
steady by the sink, reach home port,
face his stranded nakedness.

2 Belgium

No one said it wasn't heavy, straining
the suitcase, and the carrying. Scottish customs
wanted to see the dark object smudging
their scanner: explosives, uncut gem,
lump of uranium, mad-cow meat, contraband
cheese, but just a stone. It was nothing
that caught anyone's eye, there on a cold,
windy hilltop at Clava Cairns, the buried bones
centered in stone circles, a moss-encrusted
celestial calendar so old it remembers
forward. What a primitive, earthly souvenir
to say they were there and still there, though
across the channel in Brussels. Back home
his daughter breaks both her legs,
he loses his job, his wife falls seriously ill.
This is how stones are called home, through the mail
accompanied by unsigned letters of apology.

3 Spice Islands

Their gods can't live in the same village,
in jungle or tropical paradise. They can't
walk down the same street, even opposite
sides, headed in opposite directions.
Their gods spit insults. The clothes
they wear are all wrong, too much
of this color, not enough to cover that.
Food is spiced to offend.
Finally, their gods can't live
on the same island in the same country.
One of them must die or leave on a ferry
to escape the piked heads, the rapes,
and when the storm pounded the strait,
only a dozen mercilessly survive.

4 Iran

Who would dare to write so rarely
that the raw words would uplift
only to imprison the reader, though
the readers in the city of Mashad
never read more than the satanic title.
A mere million dollars is not enough
for a writing life, as if any largess
could offer us more than the time being.
Now five hundred citizens have proffered
their kidneys, right or left, the difference
unimportant, to increase a life's bounty.
The tolling already rung for publishers,
translators, and booksellers. Oh God,
what price is paid to stop another page
from being written in this phenomenal world.

5 USA

We've always known that we are all one
though mathematicians argue we could
be as far apart as six degrees of one,
where the sum of one's relationships quickly
reaches billions, yet we still don't know
the name of the person in the seat next
to us on the plane. So I really know some
one, who knows some one, who knows
some one, and so on, until the chief
of a wandering band of Kalihara Bushman
and Winona Ryder are my confidants.
So too are Elvis, the sequined king,
and Jimmy, the retired 39th president,
sixth cousins, going back to the daughter
of a 17th century German immigrant.
The White House and Graceland freely
commingling, so at the news conference
the president, in a deep and hurting voice,
sings "love me tender, love me sweet,"
and we recall that kings are best remembered.

How He Died

It was years later,
maybe three, maybe five,
after he climbed the sheer
vertical granite that rose
a thousand feet above
the mountainous gravel
road and the torrent
of snowmelt flooding
the creek, near where I
stood and watched.
He wore only tennis shoes,
rosin bag, and red silk
shorts—without ropes,
only the grip of his hands
and braided muscle of
his legs. I looked away
once at a water ouzel
pumping up and down
on a water-smoothed
boulder before it dove
and flew below the rapids.
So agile, he was nearly
to the top when I glanced
up when the canyon
detonated with thunder,
was obscured by rain,
and he continued
to climb into the clouds.

Problems with the Holy

Civilized Sacrifice

I have climbed the backs of gods too. It's not so
strange, dressed in heavy coat and boots, hat
pulled down to the eyebrows, cheeks windburnt,
gloved fingers numb, and each brief breath prayed

upon, each step thrown onto the loose altar of stone.
Blinded by spires of light, I've looked away
as the unblemished blue splintered in all directions.
And I've backed away from the sheer

precipice, the infinite suddenly a fearful measure,
the way down to tundra and the jagged maze of
granite, leaving only a crevice in which to cower.
I've lain on the steep slopes of night under spruce,

wrapped against rain and cold, and watched clouds
explode in my face. Stark boughs reached
then sagged back in a sweeping, resolute silence.
I was shaken loose by thunder and lightning,

like the small girl, named Juanita by strangers.
She tumbled a hundred yards down
Nevado Ampato peak, her whereabouts unquestioned
for five hundred years until a nearby volcano

began a festering eruption, thawing the slope,
and wrapped in her *illiclia* shawl woven in the ancient
Cuzco tradition, wearing a toucan- and parrot-
 feathered
headdress, her frozen fetal posture a last effort

at warmth above tree line amid ice fields, there
to address and redress for rain and maize, for
full vats of fermenting beer, plentiful llama herds,
for the civilized sacrifice, to be buried alive and wait

in private, as we all do to speak with our gods, hoping
to appease, to know, to secure the illusive cosmic
machinery, and in that last numb moment her left
hand gripped her dress for the intervening centuries.

Minor Gods

Another roadside bomb, another suicide
bomber, another dozen blind-folded, hands-tied-
behind-the-back bodies found half buried at the town
dump—it's how a Saturday explodes until I turn off
the radio and look out the east window at a tabby
crouched in explosive morning light and acting strangely.

I hurry outside to rescue an eight-inch long, pencil-thin,
ring-neck snake before it is playfully eviscerated.
A hundred yards into the woods, the palm heat
of cupped hands has pacified its coiled panic
and I scold it to be more careful before it calmly
slithers into a brush pile and into another ambush.

Balanced between two flood lights on the west wall,
phoebes again build a nest out of moss and spittle,
and I build a four-feet high fence on the ground below them.
They quickly abandon their efforts as if not understanding
what I'm trying to keep out and keep in. Occasionally,
I see their bobbing drab-gray tails on a nearby branch.

I leave the fence standing. I blame the cats
without evidence of guilt. Weeks later,
the phoebes return, the same pair or different,
I don't know after so many seasons of failed attempts
on every wall of the house, including the black snake
that scaled ten feet of siding to eat the hatchlings.

From the kitchen window, I watch them fly back
and forth through the gauntlet of clawed hunger,
too early to know ends except this flying.
Either the gods are omnipotent and not good,
according to Epicurius, just look at this world, or they are
good and not omnipotent, look at these phoebes.

Dialects

By the garden gate,
a robin perched
next to the windowless
wall of a house comfortable
in its disrepair. Its face turned
away from its shadow,
alert to winter's fading,
now that dock and dandelion
are sprouting. This bird
that every child recognizes,

survives factories and BB guns,
sings in a dialect,
so it too cannot stray far
from this yard before becoming
a stranger's music.
The white-crowned sparrow,
lost among cedars at the edge
of a field bleached by so much
cold light, sings a long dropping
final note, a single dialect
of grief that it carries north,
as creeks froth and rumors
of leaves start up again.

How will this small boy,
who flutters from alley to street,
over small ponds of sunlight
floating in pieces of glass,
over hilly shadows of shattered
bricks and stone, who watches
smoke abandon his city
and mailboxes fall open,
how will he ever believe me
when I whisper of another life?

How will I believe myself
but to say robin, sparrow?

Sparrows

They are alert to danger, life and death a score
simply kept by beaked heads bobbing up and down
among scattered seeds. They flock on the small concrete
basketball court beside the house—its symmetry at odds
with a field crowded and burnished purple by stalks
of broomsedge and the shrinking geography of crusted snow.
Sparrows randomly rearrange themselves, unless hunger
is an order, flying back and forth between barbed wire
fence and buck brush. Back after a night of subzero
temperatures, there is desperation in their search,
eyeing the crouched housecat, as if it were nothing more
than a misplaced shadow shaken loose from its light,
the hungry welcoming winter's early end.

Much as the cargo planes that left the secret airfields
of Buenos Aires, decades ago, during the "Dirty War,"
that leveled off far out and high over the windswept Atlantic,
and there, which is nowhere that is known or can be found again,
students and union activists, teachers and artists,
were shoved through open doors, the whole world
their flyway as they flew into the face of their beliefs,
what they'd held onto in cold cells, strapped to tables and chairs,
against cigarette burns and electric shock, and questions
never meant to be answered. Surprised, they spiraled
down, arms and legs spread, that they could not perch
on the air, and before they could consider other possibilities,
they plunged through their wet shadows.

Charles Lindbergh, first pilot to fly solo across
the Atlantic, his plane, The Spirit of St. Louis, hangs from
the ceiling of Lambert Field Terminal, its glistening body
catching the thousand eyes of travelers rushing to the next
flight—his son also disappeared, kidnapped and killed—
he said, ". . . if I had to choose, I would rather have birds
than airplanes." Today mothers, thousands of miles
away and years later, hold up placards, wear pictures
of their sons and daughters hanging from their wrinkled open

necks, the glossy photos shining in the sunlight,
all that's left as they gather each week without fail,
though some have already grown too old to ever forget
or return to the Plaza de Mayo in Buenos Aires—
but they too agree with birds, with sparrows.

This, That, or the Other

1

The sun slips an imperceptible
degree south.
Shadows stretch oaks
along the road to the breaking point,

falling off one flat earthen
edge. The blunt green
leaves, a gathering
transparency, having given

up their orioles and blackbirds
jumping between branches.
They follow clouds down
into puddle-filled ruts.

2

What's the difference blaming
the deaths of three pilots
on birds, any birds, probably
Canada or snow geese flying

along the front range of mountains,
though it's never mentioned
at the press conference except
to ask if this is common,

and whether there were screens
over the engines, and the suggestion
that something more could
be done. The officer

rules out the option
of "getting rid of all the birds,"
as if it had been considered,
might be possible.

3

Luminous maples light
the evening road, Virginia
creeper wraps the trunks
of sycamores like the exposed

arteries in an anatomy
text, the scarlet ladders
of sumac climb in all directions,
a willow by the creek

explodes, its leaves falling
into chilled grasses. There are
innuendoes: the wind, the season,
sonic boom, the official view.

Photographing the Wind

> All photographs are accurate.
> None of them is truth.
> —Richard Avedon

This is a wholly comfortable wind,
tailored and too expensive for the end
of a ragged century. Sitting on the porch,
it has us believing again. I breathe
this wind that isn't in a hurry,
isn't pushing through the crowd
of oaks to see what has fallen, isn't
banging unlatched screen doors to get in,
isn't rattling loose panes awake,
isn't scooping up newspapers and forcing
their headlines against fences; it's already
too late. We drink coffee, balance
cups on the wooden railing and forget.

The bird in the photograph has already
abandoned the air and stands
on barren ground, a lord with wings
folded, statuesque, a feathered black
granite that has dropped from an African
sky. Though the bird looms large
and too alert, it's in the background,
and on this all too clear and sunny day
we know the bird can't be blamed.
This is simply what it knows best.
Though it may have arrived a little
early, it is certain in its waiting.

The naked child, has drawn her knees up
to her chest, her forehead pressed against
years of parched ground, her forearms
stretched forward and away from either side
of her thinning body, her back to the steadfast bird,
guardian of this warring, drought-stricken plain.

This is when we want to believe in a wind
such as this one crossing the porch,
that refuses to carry a cry or spread
the scent of finality, and instead braids
strands of warmth through the cool
of evening, between the spaces of outspread
fingers, our hands failed kites,
our lives falling through this luxurious air.

The Freight of Parakeets

The windows are closed.
The glass smudged with breath.
It's late winter or early spring.
The forward seats of the passenger car
are occupied by soldiers.
It could be the beginning
of another war when victory
is believable, or the middle
when there is still hope.
In the railroad station,
I climbed steps to enter a high darkness
and felt my way to an empty seat.
I carry a delicate wire cage draped
in a blanket. Smoke from cigarettes
spins through dim lights.
I can't really see them
except for their campaign hats
draped over back-seat rests.
Each story is followed
by the clink of flasks.
Once hats are thrown into
the air, but I'm too young
and tired to listen.
I lie on my side across two seats,
curl my legs around
the cage behind my knees.
A small high-pitched singing
stops all the joking; a bird's song
that's out of place, out of this world,
but in this car. Faces hollowed
with shadows look up and down
the aisle. The train rocks
and rattles. The hulk of a passing
freight smears the window.

The Right Nurture, The Left Nature

Maybe it's on the level of pulling wings
off flies at five years old, or firing
ants into dance under a magnifying glass,
all in the name of young science.

Decades later, that's how we reason
these tiny tortures, and just the other day
stepping off the curb, I followed
the scientific method, noticing that I led

with my right foot, and after jaywalking
and forcing a car to slow down, I stepped
over the curb to cross the street, leading
with my right foot again. Is this Archimedian,

no matter how I alternated my approach
to the stairs, should I say stars,
and how oddly stuttered my switching of steps,
it's my right foot that ends up on the first tread.

Only if I stop and place my left foot on the curb
or stair or star can I begin my journey work of a
        thousand
miles differently. I must look like a human
hiccup, skipping along, leading with right foot

twice then three times with my left. Blake
swore his Miltonic inspiration came through
his left foot. He showed the hair burned
off his toes to prove it, but he always kept

his right foot shoed. I wonder, on which foot
armies start their marching? Could we slow
them down, change their direction,
get them dancing, if they switched feet?

Flight Lessons

"Crito, I owe a cock to Asclepius;
will you remember to pay the debt."
                    —Socrates

Months high in the Carpathian Mountains,
his legs feel unreal without skis. He's ready
to believe his body blue, his skin meant

to peel. A hissing snow sheds cold scales
over those peaks. He's patiently absorbed
in the fierce calculations of ambush

when he's captured in a white uniform
in a green forest. He stands in a serpentine line
amid hills of fuming sawdust. The line grows shorter.

The prisoners prodded by guards who hold
them down by their shoulders before the sawmill's blade.
Heads mushroom in fairy rings over the frozen dirt.

Two men ahead of him when shells explode.
The guards dive under wagons corded
with headless bodies. He runs, swims an ice-choked river.

His medals framed on a wall in a farmhouse that was once half
barn, where chickens roosted in the rafters
and cows slept on the other side of the bedroom wall.

The attic is haunted on windy nights by scratching.
An old woman hobbles into the yard,
the sum of world wars, inflation, depression.

She deftly throttles an unsuspecting chicken,
carries it squawking to the chopping block.
In one motion she wrings its neck and swings

the hatchet with a quick twist. Its head pops off.
The feathered heap, legs frantic,
claws the bare ground. Clownish, acrobatic,

the body leaps forward then flips onto its back,
wings beating against bare ground.
He never mentioned men flapping their arms.

Angelic Longings

Beside the empty plates the folded wings of angels.
The scepters of knife, fork, and spoon lie on the table.
The diner's etiquette calls for feathers to be dabbed at the corners
of mouths. Lipstick and gravy trace the zenith of flight.
Wings fluttering across laps are the zeitgeist of arousal, reason

enough for these cravings. A few guests still don't understand,
become uneasy when a hand reaches under the table to caress
their angelic longings. The table cloth rich with spilled burgundy,
traces the borders of intoxicated continents that wait to be explored
by a pair of fallen tongues, and later with the soft panting of wings.

Here insulated angels hold up the heated corners of hell
and a flaming fondue. They keep vigil by the oven door
to escort a roasted soul to the carving block. In the living
room, the crowd grows anxious. Between the sofa
and ceiling, Saint Albert tallies four hundred million

of the wingéd. Cabalists wearing zircon rings agree.
One wet white blur works the four thousand nine hundred
names of God. Another is half fire, half ice.
The spooked guests begin to think angels everywhere,
even converting the kitchen witch. No matter how

humble and discrete the conception, because the guests
can think of God at all, must mean there is God.
They'll argue details and style over another glass
of Pinot Grigio. On the radio by the couch, it's reported
an artillery shell exploded in the crowded market

of a besieged city. Sirens wailed loudly through the air
for hours. Because men can conceive of death, they have
become its overheated engine. In the dining room no one is
listening. Saint Albert employs the Heimlich on the host
choking on a buffalo wing, her face turning angelic blue.

Breakneck Speed

Weighing, measuring, calculating,
a cloudy Sunday he trims the grass.
His wife pushes the mower, counting
bags of clippings lined along the driveway
like the slumped-over executed.

Drenched and puddled, interminable gray days
follow. A black umbrella clenched
in praying hands, a devout pedestrian's
weathering sepulcher. Slipping into a theater,
the celluloid fields last hours,
not the desperate, dry, desired days.

A book unfolds into a flotilla of paper boats
that sail through the room. Beginning, middle,
end drift past each other in a rudderless story.
The buoy of worry bobs over the obese
murderer on death row. Lawyers claim

he's too heavy to be hanged, hanging
would result in beheading, beheading
cruel if not unusual. From the table
of headless calculations, the state
argues chances for head loss are no more
than usual on a rainy day.

Superman's Suicide

Early evening, cars and trucks crowd
the interstate with speed. Lingering yellow
light candles the single row of trees
around the hotel's parking lot, blinding west
bound traffic, igniting sparks on windshields
and chrome. Outside the fifth floor window,
a man takes aim at the world, he's threatening
to blow a hole wide enough to fly through.
Ignore that he hasn't written a note,
pointed any fingers, laid any blame—
his plans are too simple and direct
to leave doubt. Ignore that he is
walking on air, that he is already
more buoyant than helium.
His gun has taken the shape of a cloud
and he struggles to grasp its diamond
grip. Each turn of the muggy breeze
blows its caliber away. Ignore that this man
is falling upward, unlike the rest of us
who rush to claim our earth, gaining
twenty miles per second when we step
off the balcony. He aims into
each window as he passes. Down
the barrel's sight, he follows his reflection.
In each room, the occupants see something
cloudy pointed at them. A few dive
behind desks and couches, hoping
to save something of their lives,
others simply die into their beds.
Are they playing, no one is certain
until morning, when they leave
the sheets stretched stiff and the blankets
neatly folded over pillows. He no longer
needs to prove man of steel more powerful
than a speeding locomotive. He squeezes the trigger.
He doesn't care, he's doomed to reruns.

Problems with the Holy

Sometimes return is all anyone wants.
—Francis Driscoll

A plane skims the treetops, angles toward the
unmown field, searching for a level place to
crash, to become another whir amid the
locusts and grasshoppers, but the single
engine is running strong. Its wings project
straight from either side of the cockpit. Fescue
and bluestem ripple in the propeller's wake.
The plane's struts knock off the bushy
seedheads of grass. This low the pilot could
name the constellations of brown-eyed
Susans and pink thistles scattered across this
green sky.

The pilot hasn't seen the Korean War
photograph of my father standing beside a
small reconnaissance plane like the one
skimming the field, crushed at the end of a
corrugated metal runway, wings and fuselage
beyond any sense of flight. Perhaps it flew
into the snowy mountain rising in the
distance, or crosshairs. I haven't seen my
father in years to ask.

On Memorial Day, in a field in the next
county, a vintage WWII fighter plows to a
stop, bellied in a sea of mud, unable to out
maneuver the old nightmare of enemy fire.
Or is it the blue canyons drifting between
towering cumulus that defies the plane's
instruments and sends the awestruck pilot
diving to escape this rarefied beauty for a
feral field.

Walking on Air

At a Glance

Near the front door on a low branch
a silhouette squawks and flies,
as if only half made for flight,
as though something medieval fell
from a lichen-stained parapet.

I guess wood duck.
So far from steady water,
I can't be sure, unlike the crows
who crowd the oaks nearly every morning,
clearing harsh throats

of their opaque presence.
Same with the wide-winged glide
of midsummer vultures, blackened
by sun, their raw heads cocking
loudly to one side as they pass

overhead. Last night, in a record
low April cold, she held a flash-
light and frantically called, hearing a tear
in the forest floor, an explosion
of leaves and a stuttering squeal.

She directed the thin beam
like a baton conducting the dark
from tree to tree, through the bushes,
searching for something
to save. Life teased into dying,

slowly she approached the cat,
calmly calling its name,
picking it up and placing it over
her shoulder as she would a child
out too late, now safe. She turned

toward the house, the flashlight pointing
down catching, one at a time, the brilliance
of her bare legs, a corner of her naked
hip, and the dark shining wing
flying up between her thighs.

Walking on Air

Blocks away, three o'clock in the morning,
the streets barricaded, the high-rise
hotel burdened by too many stories

of satin, chauffeurs, floodlights, and in closing,
the entropy of burlap, crushed butts, turned
tricks. Beginning, end, carefully dynamited.

Detonation and windows trembled with a secret
falling excitement. For less than a breath,
walls of concrete and brick stood on dust.

What brought us to this precise implosion
when the brown cloud swelled
hundreds of feet into the air, rushing

the streets, dirt swallowing the windowed
canyons between buildings, streetlights
submerged into a jaundice far below?

I think we had tried all evening, our hands
kneading soft the masonry of each other's bodies,
but the walls were not ravaged so exactingly.

Still the room stood oddly open, as doubt
built its own thick-walled house. We contrived
to watch the blur settle, leaving a film on sill

and glass that from the inside our fingers
could not reach to write the necessary words.
Thin grimy ridges of accumulation

began to avalanche into dry tears. We tapped
the pane on the eleventh floor,
trying to attract anyone's passing attention.

The Landing

She walked barefoot on the gravel road
past the shirtless boys tossing and stacking
hay bales on a flatbed truck idling
in the middle of a field, past a neighbor's house,
no one at home but their chained baying
redbone hounds, then she turned into the driveway
of a man puzzling in front of the opened hood
of his pickup, where she stepped naked
onto the fender, climbed over the grille
to sit, Aphrodite rising on his engine's air filter.
He sent his two teenage boys into the house,
their eager faces crowding the kitchen window.
He didn't hesitate when he told the oldest
to telephone the man living by the pond,
who quickly arrived to escort her back,
a greasy handprint on her left buttock.

Later that day she would decide to fly,
and she did, if down is flight and not simply
falling featherless, when she jumped
from the balcony above the atrium
and caught one corner of the cast-iron wood stove
with her hip. A flowerpot-sized bruise
blossomed almost instantly, and would
transform from hydrangea to hibiscus to mimosa
until wilting back to pale flesh a month later.

Earlier that day, she opened the refrigerator,
and using two quarts of strawberries smeared
all the windows on the first floor of the house,
the world now as she saw it, rosy and melting.
Finally, she lay down on the porch,

where he covered her with a blanket
so that she might find her breasts, her spine,
her hair, where she expected upon landing.

—for Jill and Larry

Southern Perfection

On the map there's a name
floating on blue.
                        He travels
to a small island, almost
too small to find.
                        The plane
plummets through a sea
of clouds. He has just left
                        his wife
though she says how can
he leave from what's never arrived.
                        He gives
up arguing and arrives at
his leaving. His first heat-
                        warped step
is into the glare of the white-
washed decay of colonial
                        mansions.
He discovers
the ocean is an ever-opening
                        vowel that
becomes thick and hot
the longer he lies in
                        the sand.
It reminds him of
his wife, the sand radiating
                        an end-
less sigh of dismissal.
Farther down the beach
                        bathers
take off their skins.
The apartment he rents
                        echoes
nightly neighborly gunshots
and a tireless steel-drum
                        music.
Though it's a stray, the cat

that already lives on
                    the porch
adopts him. Days later
he finds it dead on
                    the stoop.
Each evening for
a week there's a tarantula
                    nailed through
its abdomen to
the door. He buys a car,
                    the side
mirror held on
with wire. The first night
                    parked in
an alley the head-
and taillights are smashed.
                    It is
a perfection, the breaking
of what's broken.

                    —for Terry Mitze

The Unmistaken

On either side of the door two dead birds:
the ravaged red male, his wings folded closed,
his body a slick flamed streak, a struck match
with nowhere to burn but darker; and the duller,
ash-brown female, her stick legs thrust out,
her wings half opened, head thrown back, propped
up by her fanned tail, standing in rigor, defiant
to her last moment, and still so. Is this another
of history's classic love affairs where desire
turns tragic no matter the innocence?
Or did he fly into a window that closed too quickly
and she followed, struggling to keep it open,
or she under siege, fought the threat, while he made
only an elegant and noble gesture in the placid way
he lay on the weathered porch, death's bold red
napkin neatly folded, but she would not surrender
to death's inevitable feast?   Is it simply foolish to believe
there is more story than accident, accident the lesser story?
It must have happened earlier today, their black eyes
already collapsed. Were they chased, or did they simply
lose sight of the air, or the house appeared
out of a dimension of forest too late to fly around?
Together by the door, an unmistakable symmetry.

Our Insect Lives:

1 Pupa

This mode of flight has nothing to do,
or very little, with bipedalism,
other than the marvelous and the fantastic,
what two hands and opposable thumbs can
only imagine and recognize in their limitations:
scratching and shaping the solid, caressing
the substantial, and only fondling the wriggling air.

2 Cocoon

It's the face of grinding boredom
as the walls thicken and ceilings sink.
We think our heads are in the clouds
and bang into a starling-stained chandelier.
Surprised and foolish, we believe we can fly
out the shattered windows. Our strategy
all along to lower the standards, disown
beak and feather, scale and proboscis,
for ailerons and afterburners.

3 Delayed Stall

The momentum of desire lost,
tailspin and free fall inevitable,
the diaphanous wings steeply angled
to catch a hint of lift to delay the stall
and beat another time
through yet another stall. That's how
our lives are lived, catching our breath
and then another, after we know too much,
the hurt burning us into pure flight,
and with ashen breath stall
back into the living.

4 Rotational Circulation

That mad insect thrumming,
that mosquito whine,
dodging the hurdling horsefly buzz,
that deafening ebb of churring cicadas,
that grasshopper crackle across scorched
August fields, it is in the rotational circulation
of manic wings, that pulling backward
at the end of each stroke that drags air
into the next—we can't help but remember
those moments when sheets clouded
the bed, fold upon urgent fold
building into a cotton cumulus,
shoved there by feet insistent upon
catapulting two bodies into flight,
and the slow moist circling,
the drawing back again, again.

5 Wake Capture

What's crawling back into the earth?
Who is there left to wake?
We must find someone who still knows.
We must not believe that the only wake
is what trails behind and is lost, no matter
how long we linger over rippling mirrors.
Must we believe that these black
suits and dull ties will save us,
or help anyone along, or hold forth
a reverence longer than sorrow.
We cannot wake anyone again.
It's our last chance to soar,
these wings moving fastly invisible,
capturing the split-second wake
of the last beat. We are thrust forward,
uplifted, sailing through each failing moment
of our momentary flights.

Breakfast with Asteroids

Two million years into the Late Pliocene,
consciousness leaps and crawls before any of us,
beyond clear beginnings of our struggle, when an asteroid
doused its fiery body in the Bellinghausen Sea,
names only we need to locate ourselves, our suffering,
amid ice sheets more blank than Locke ever imagined.
The splash went three miles in the air, sent a tidal
wave twelve stories high into the Pacific Rim,
and perhaps rained unnamed creatures on the Transantarctic
Mountains, explaining the "Sirius enigma." Another
sixty-five million years back, an asteroid crashed
into Yucatan leaving a crater wider then the sprawl
of Los Angeles, dust blotting out the sun, extincting
three-quarters of all species—too early for us to worry.

This morning I've a headache. I've collided with at least
the meteor responsible for the mile-wide crater in Arizona—
six hundred feet deep when it stopped, but I'm plunging deeper.
For weeks now, I've been dreaming that the trees are still
burning with light. I remember looking out the window,
astonished that after so many killing frosts,
that so many oaks are still green and rustling
with wind. Is it the lifting of a dish, then a
glass, then a fork, out of soapy water, wiping
them with washrag and rinsing, then setting
them on the rack to drain, these stark daily details,
what the living do, that sends me
plummeting through another barren season?
The trees leafless, the sink empty.

Red Shift

If you lost something red on Tuesday,
    as the sign taped to the west entrance
door asks, it must not be the Coke machine
    thrumming its one tune, change
rattling in its throat, cans rolling off
    its tongue–thirst always glowing
at the end of a long dark hallway.
    It's not the exit signs above every
door, warning us not to stay too long,
    that this way is the way out
when necessity arrives as it always does,
    but if we look down another hallway
there's a sign claiming its the way out,
    in rain, in sunshine.
It's certainly not the fire extinguisher,
    recessed into the wall, where it sits
all day behind glass, a museum of our
    incinerating fears, waiting for us
to rediscover our own or someone else's
    emergency and then to break
the glass with a fist or spiked heel
    and appear out of the smoke a hero
or in ashes. Perhaps it's a simple
    misunderstanding of how celestial
bodies travel vast hallways, not realizing
    that as we move away from each other,
the distance squares the speed squaring
    the distance, that light shifts across
the spectrum toward longer wavelengths
    and all that is left is a red glow,
what is found of your leaving,
    so even if you did lose something
red on Tuesday, as the sign asks,
    we can't call back this universe.

Scorched

All of humanity's problems stem
from man's inability to sit in a room alone.
                                        —Pascal

The room's too long, the walls curved.
We are squeezed shoulder to shoulder,
cheek to jowl, smell to odor.

Soon we will leave some of this behind.
Not the crying baby who redreams wings.
Soon we will skip over the air.

We, the adults, resort to making lists
for later today, the day after tomorrow.
The quotidian can't wait for us

to show up as proof
with the next plan to fix the breakage
or be lulled far afield into indifferent pieces.

Flung back in our seats,
the pressure presses us
into flight. Steep banking

as we turn to head west, windows
at our feet, we are ready to jump
into that spilled glitter

of scattered lakes, shifting ribbons
of rivers, contoured lines of farms.
We lose ourselves in clouds,

find our winged shadow suspended
in mists, racing across snow-dusted
mesas, vast salt pans. We pray for smoke,

the blue incense of tires scorching
runways. We deplane, passengers
plainly ready for that plain room.

Walter Bargen has published ten books of poems, including *Harmonic Balance* (2001), *The Body of Water* (2003), and *The Feast* (2004). His poems and fictions have appeared in over one hundred magazines, including *American Literary Review*, *American Letters & Commentary*, *Beloit Poetry Journal*, *Denver Quarterly*, *Georgia Review*, *Missouri Review*, *New Letters*, *New Novel Review*, *Pleiades*, *Poetry East*, *River Styx*, *Seneca Review*, *Sycamore Review*, and *Witness*. He is the recipient of a National Endowment for the Arts poetry fellowship (1991); winner of the Hanks Prize (1995), Quarter After Eight Prose Prize (1996), the Chester H. Jones Foundation poetry prize (1997), and the William Rockhill Nelson Award (2005).

Printed in the United States
57364LVS00003B/226-228

9 781933 456409